D1252680

MIGHTY MACHINES IN ACTION

Zamboni®
Ice Resurfacers

by Rebecca Pettiford

ZAMBONI

BLASTOFF! 2 READERS

BELLWETHER MEDIA • MINNEAPOLIS, MN

Note to Librarians, Teachers, and Parents:

Blastoff! Readers are carefully developed by literacy experts and combine standards-based content with developmentally appropriate text.

Level 1 provides the most support through repetition of high-frequency words, light text, predictable sentence patterns, and strong visual support.

Level 2 offers early readers a bit more challenge through varied simple sentences, increased text load, and less repetition of high-frequency words.

Level 3 advances early-fluent readers toward fluency through increased text and concept load, less reliance on visuals, longer sentences, and more literary language.

Level 4 builds reading stamina by providing more text per page, increased use of punctuation, greater variation in sentence patterns, and increasingly challenging vocabulary.

Level 5 encourages children to move from "learning to read" to "reading to learn" by providing even more text, varied writing styles, and less familiar topics.

Whichever book is right for your reader, Blastoff! Readers are the perfect books to build confidence and encourage a love of reading that will last a lifetime!

This edition first published in 2018 by Bellwether Media, Inc.

No part of this publication may be reproduced in whole or in part without written permission of the publisher. For information regarding permission, write to Bellwether Media, Inc., Attention: Permissions Department, 5357 Penn Avenue South, Minneapolis, MN 55419.

Library of Congress Cataloging-in-Publication Data

Names: Pettiford, Rebecca, author.
Title: Zamboni Ice Resurfacers / by Rebecca Pettiford.
Description: Minneapolis, MN : Bellwether Media, Inc., [2018] | Series: Blastoff! Readers. Mighty Machines in Action | Includes bibliographical references and index. | Audience: Grades K-3. | Audience: Ages 5-8.
Identifiers: LCCN 2016052958 (print) | LCCN 2016055668 (ebook) | ISBN 9781626176348 (hardcover : alk. paper) | ISBN 9781681033648 (ebook)
Subjects: LCSH: Zamboni Ice Resurfacers (Trademark)–Juvenile literature. | Skating rinks–Equipment and supplies–Juvenile literature.Classification: LCC GV852 .P48 2018 (print) | LCC GV852 (ebook) | DDC 796.91028/4–dc23
LC record available at https://lccn.loc.gov/2016052958

Editor: Christina Leighton   Designer: Steve Porter

Printed in the United States of America, North Mankato, MN.

Table of

SMOOTH SKATING

A horn blares. It is time for hockey players to leave the ice rink.

Soon, a Zamboni ice resurfacer appears.

The driver moves the Zamboni machine slowly around the ice rink.

The machine cleans the ice in minutes. Now the hockey game can continue!

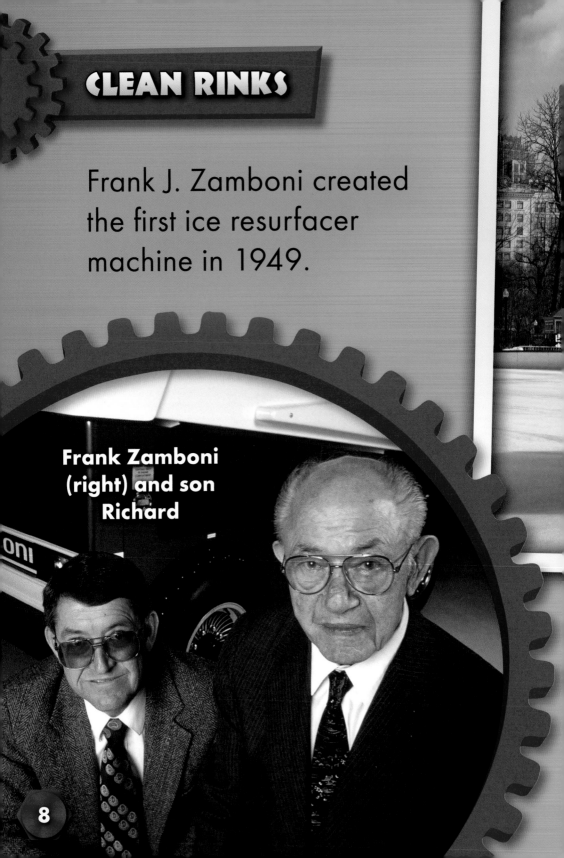

CLEAN RINKS

Frank J. Zamboni created the first ice resurfacer machine in 1949.

Frank Zamboni (right) and son Richard

He wanted a fast way to make ice rinks clean and smooth. Today, Zamboni machines clean up indoor and outdoor rinks.

conditioner

Each Zamboni machine has a **conditioner** in back.

The conditioner holds many important parts for cleaning the ice.

ZAMBONI® ICE RESURFACER
SIZE
Zamboni® Model 526

height: 7.2 feet (2.2 meters)

average human

length: 13.1 feet (4 meters)

The conditioner has a long, sharp **blade** that shaves the ice.

MACHINE PROFILE
ZAMBONI® MODEL 500

speed: 9.7 miles (15.6 kilometers) per hour

quarter mile time: 93.5 seconds

snow tank

ZAMBONI

screws

Then **screws** collect the shaved ice. They push the ice into a snow tank in front.

Next, the machine washes the ice. The water comes from a wash tank.

wash tank

A **squeegee** in the conditioner wipes up the dirty ice and water.

Lastly, the Zamboni machine sprays the rink with warm water.

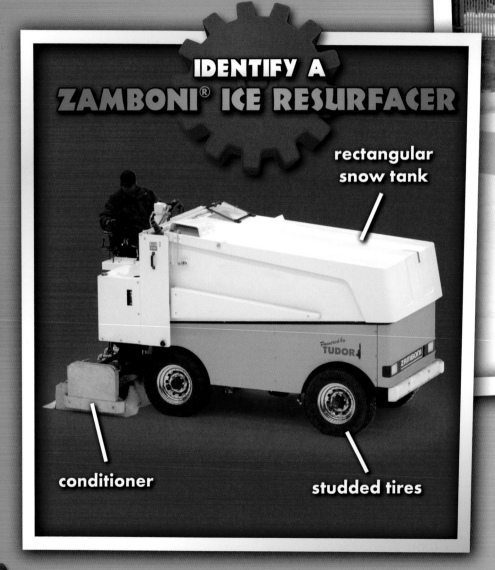

IDENTIFY A ZAMBONI® ICE RESURFACER

rectangular snow tank

conditioner

studded tires

towel

A towel spreads the water. The water **freezes** and makes the rink smooth and safe to skate on!

ICE MASTERS

Some Zamboni machines run on **electricity**. Others use **fuel**.

CANTON-POTSDAM
HOSPITAL
CARING BEYOND MEDICINE

GO KNIGHTS!

ZAMBONI

studded tires

Studded tires keep the machines from sliding as they power forward.

A Zamboni ice resurfacer only takes a few minutes to clean the ice.

Soon, the smooth ice rink
is ready for skaters!

Glossary

blade—a large metal plate that works like a shovel

conditioner—the back part of an ice resurfacer that stores most of its tools

electricity—energy carried through wires

freezes—becomes cold and hard

fuel—a material burned to make heat or power

screws—simple machines made of twisted metal that can move shaved ice up or down

squeegee—a rubber strip used for spreading water and other liquids

studded—having small metal or rubber pieces sticking out all over

To Learn More

AT THE LIBRARY

Kulling, Monica. *Clean Sweep! Frank Zamboni's Ice Machine.* New York, N.Y.: Tundra Books, 2016.

McMullan, Kate and Jim. *I'm Cool!* New York, N.Y.: Balzer + Bray, 2015.

Olson, Kay Melchisedech. *Frank Zamboni and the Ice-Resurfacing Machine.* Mankato, Minn.: Capstone Press, 2008.

ON THE WEB

Learning more about Zamboni ice resurfacers is as easy as 1, 2, 3.

1. Go to www.factsurfer.com.

2. Enter "Zamboni ice resurfacers" into the search box.

3. Click the "Surf" button and you will see a list of related web sites.

With factsurfer.com, finding more information is just a click away.

Index